What is
touch?

SUN SCREEN
25 SPF

Molly Aloian

🌴 Crabtree Publishing Company
www.crabtreebooks.com

Author
Molly Aloian

Publishing plan research and development
Sean Charlebois, Reagan Miller
Crabtree Publishing Company

Editorial director
Kathy Middleton

Editor
Crystal Sikkens

Proofreader
Kelly McNiven

Design
Samara Parent

Photo research
Crystal Sikkens, Samara Parent

Production coordinator
and prepress technician
Samara Parent

Print coordinator
Katherine Berti

Photographs
Thinkstock: pages 7, 9, 14, 22 (keys, slippers, pencil)
All other images by Shutterstock

Library and Archives Canada Cataloguing in Publication

Aloian, Molly
   What is touch? / Molly Aloian.

(Senses close-up)
Includes index.
Issued also in electronic format.
ISBN 978-0-7787-0968-8 (bound).--ISBN 978-0-7787-0991-6 (pbk.)

   1. Touch--Juvenile literature. I. Title. II. Series: Senses close-up

QP451.A56 2013   j612.8'8   C2013-901616-3

Library of Congress Cataloging-in-Publication Data

CIP available at Library of Congress

Crabtree Publishing Company

www.crabtreebooks.com   1-800-387-7650

Printed in the U.S.A./042013/SX20130306

Published in Canada
Crabtree Publishing
616 Welland Ave.
St. Catharines, Ontario
L2M 5V6

Published in the United States
Crabtree Publishing
PMB 59051
350 Fifth Avenue, 59th Floor
New York, New York 10118

Published in the United Kingdom
Crabtree Publishing
Maritime House
Basin Road North, Hove
BN41 1WR

Published in Australia
Crabtree Publishing
3 Charles Street
Coburg North
VIC 3058

Contents

Your sense of touch

Touch is one of your five main senses. You use it every day along with your sense of hearing, taste, smell, and sight. Each of your senses give you information about the things around you. You learn a lot about your surroundings by using your senses.

Your skin

You feel and touch things with your skin. Skin covers most of your body. Take a moment to feel what is touching your skin right now. What do you feel?

What do you think?

Why do we need our five senses?

Feeling your way

Your sense of touch allows you to feel all kinds of things. It lets you feel an object's temperature. For example, a cup of hot chocolate will feel warm in your hands. A glass of ice water feels cold.

What do you think?

What parts of the body help us feel and touch?

Feel it

You can also feel whether things are rough or smooth.

You can feel whether something is hard, sharp, or soft.

You can feel if something is wet or dry.

Your skin

You have skin all over your body. Your skin is your body's largest **organ**. It covers your body and stretches as you move around. It is like a protective covering. It stops harmful things from getting into your body.

No matter how you move, your skin stretches with you.

The skin you are in

Your skin helps control the temperature of your body. If you are too hot, your skin releases water called **sweat** to cool you down. Your skin also helps to keep heat inside your body if you are too cold.

You lose water through your skin when you sweat. It is important to replace the water you have lost.

Three layers

You have three main layers of skin. There is an outer layer and two inner layers. The protective outer layer is called the **epidermis**. It is made up of dead **cells**. These dead cells fall off and get replaced by new cells.

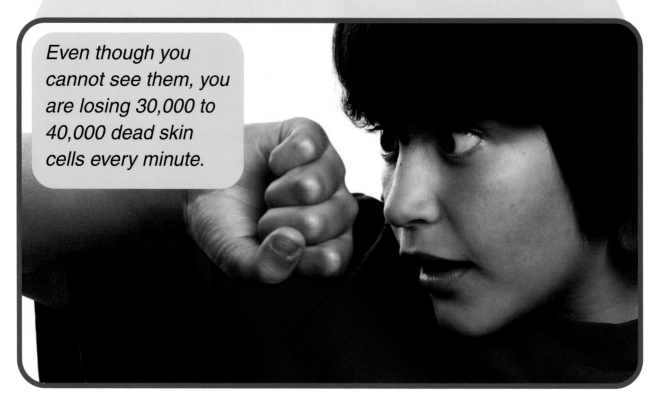

Even though you cannot see them, you are losing 30,000 to 40,000 dead skin cells every minute.

Inner layers

The layer under the epidermis is called the **dermis**. It contains **nerves** with **sensory receptors**. The receptors let you feel the objects you touch. The **hypodermis** is the bottom layer. It is made up of fat that helps keep you warm.

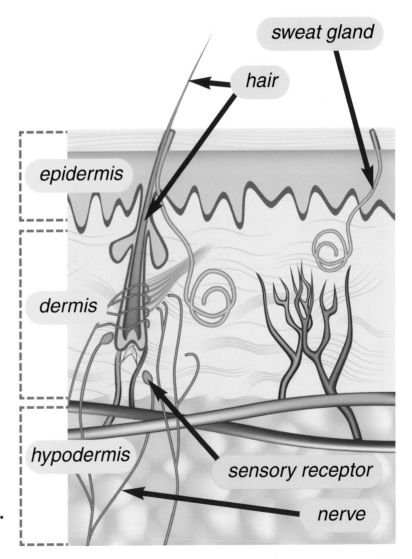

sweat gland

hair

epidermis

dermis

hypodermis

sensory receptor

nerve

11

Sending messages

When you touch something, nerves send messages to your brain right away. Your brain then tells you what you are feeling.

Skin sensors

At the end of each nerve is a sensory receptor that can sense things like pressure, pain, hot, and cold. Each receptor only reacts to a certain feeling. For example, some receptors let you feel pain. Others tell you if something is hot or cold.

What do you think?

Which receptors react when you scrape your arm?

Sensitive skin

Certain parts of your skin are more sensitive than others. This is because these parts have more nerve endings, or receptors. The skin on your lips, fingertips, and toes is the most sensitive. The skin on your back and on your bottom is less sensitive.

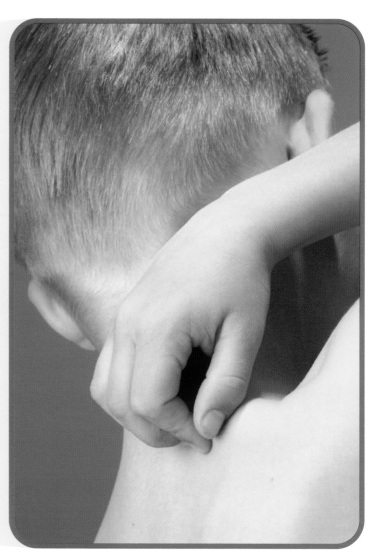

Tickle, tickle

Your feet or the back of your neck tend to have a lot of receptors that react to a light touch. This makes these spots ticklish when someone touches them.

What do you think?

What parts of your body are the most ticklish? Why do you think this is?

Animals touch, too

Animals can touch, too. Animals such as cats, hamsters, and rabbits also feel their surroundings. They use their whiskers to feel. Their whiskers tell them if a space is big enough for them to fit through.

whiskers

hamster

Sharks can feel movements as far as 300 feet (91 meters) away.

Feeling prey

Sharks have tiny holes on their faces and along the sides of their bodies. These holes let the sharks feel small movements in the water. This helps them find **prey**.

Touch is important

Your sense of touch helps you learn about what is going on around you. It helps keep you safe. If a cup feels hot, the drink inside may be too hot to drink. Your sense of touch can also help you in a fire. If a door feels hot, the fire could be on the other side. So, it is not safe to go out that way.

Reading with fingers

People who are **blind** can read books, signs, and other things by feeling patterns of small bumps with their fingers. This is called **Braille**. They are using their sense of touch to read.

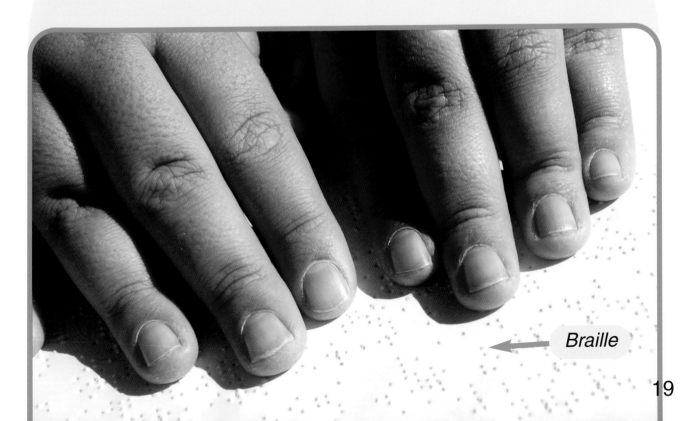

Braille

Protect your skin

It is important to protect your skin from very hot and cold temperatures that can damage your sense of touch. Sharp, pointy objects can cut your skin. When you get a cut, part of your protective epidermis layer of skin is removed. This means dirt can then get to your inner layers of skin.

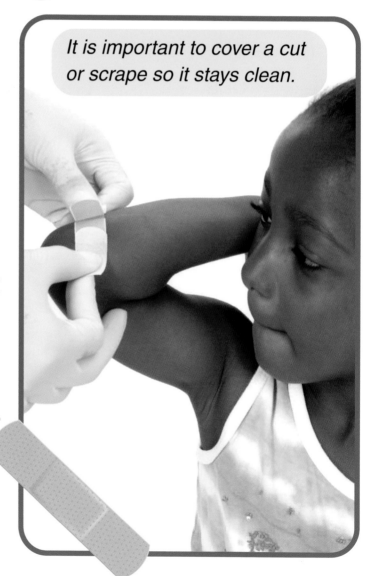

It is important to cover a cut or scrape so it stays clean.

Cover up

Too much sunshine can be dangerous. It can burn your skin. Be sure to wear **sunscreen** if you are outside on a sunny day. Always cover your skin if you are outside during cold winter weather.

What do you think?

What can you wear to protect your skin in cold weather?

Touch test

How much can you find out by using your sense of touch? This activity will help show you. You will need:

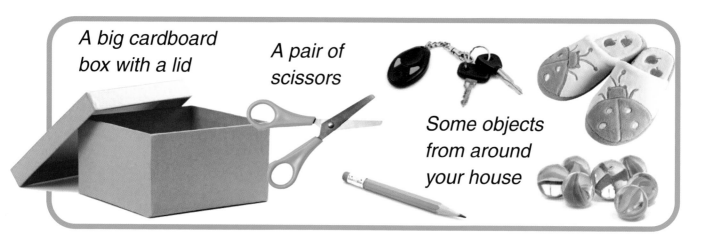

A big cardboard box with a lid

A pair of scissors

Some objects from around your house

1. Ask an adult to help you cut two holes in the box that are big enough to put your hands through.
2. Have a friend close their eyes while you put an object from around your house in the box.
3. Have your friend put their hands through the holes and touch the object. Did he or she guess what it was?
4. Replace it with another object.
5. Write down which objects your friend guessed correctly.

Learning more

Books

What is Touch? (Lightning Bolt Books: Your Amazing Senses)
    by Jennifer Boothroyd. Lerner Publications, 2009.

My Senses Help Me (My World) by Bobbie Kalman.
    Crabtree Publishing Company, 2010.

How Touch Works (Our Senses) by Sally Morgan.
    Powerkids Press, 2010.

Touching (The Five Senses) by Rebecca Rissman.
    Heinemann-Raintree, 2010.

Websites

Your Sense of Touch
http://library.thinkquest.org/3750/touch/touch.html

All About Your Senses: Experiments to Try
http://kidshealth.org/kid/closet/experiments/experiment_main.html

Sid the Science Kid
http://pbskids.org/sid/isense.html

Words to know

Note: Some boldfaced words are defined where they appear in the book.

blind (blahynd) adjective Unable to see

Braille (breyl) noun A kind of writing for the blind in which raised dots stand for letters

cells (selz) noun The millions of tiny building blocks that make up your body

nerves (nurvz) noun Thin strings of tissue in your body that carry messages to and from your brain

organ (AWR-guhn) noun An important body part that is made up of cells and tissues

prey (prey) noun Animals that are hunted and eaten by other animals

sensory receptor (SEN-suh-ree ri-SEP-ter) noun The ending of a nerve that senses hot, cold, pain, or pressure and sends messages to your brain

sunscreen (SUHN-skreen) noun Lotion that stops you from getting burnt by the Sun

sweat (swet) noun Liquid that comes out of tiny holes in your skin

A noun is a person, place, or thing. An adjective is a word that tells you what something is like.

Index